ROGER GOWER

SPEAKING

UPPER – INTERMEDIATE

OXFORD SUPPLEMENTARY SKILLS

SERIES EDITOR: ALAN MALEY

OXFORD UNIVERSITY PRESS

Oxford University Press
Walton Street, Oxford OX2 6DP

Oxford New York Toronto Madrid
Delhi Bombay Calcutta Madras Karachi
Kuala Lumpur Singapore Hong Kong Tokyo
Nairobi Dar es Salaam Cape Town
Melbourne Auckland

and associated companies in
Berlin Ibadan

Oxford and *Oxford English* are trade marks of
Oxford University Press

ISBN 0 19 453412 X

© Oxford University Press 1987

First published 1987
Fourth impression 1993

Set by Promenade Graphics Ltd, Cheltenham.

Printed in Hong Kong

Illustrations by:

Karen Daws
David Haldane
John Helms
Punch Publications Ltd
John Ridgway
Susan Scott

The publishers would like to thank the following for
permission to reproduce photographs:

BBC Hulton Picture Library
Beken of Cowes
Bridgeman Art Library
Jane Davies
Eastern Daily Press
Mary Evans
Network
Rex Features
Topham
Trustees of the National Gallery, London
Usborne Publishing Ltd

ACKNOWLEDGEMENTS

I would like to thank the following: Margaret Pearson and Alan Pulverness for some of the ideas; Ruth Dendy for her secretarial assistance; and the students of the Bell School of Languages, Cambridge for trying out the exercises.

Acknowledgements are also made to the following writers and publishers who have allowed us to use material that falls within their copyright:

Dino Buzzati and John Calder Ltd for the outline of the short story 'The Landslide' from *Catastrophe and other Short Stories* (Calder & Boyars Ltd 1965); L.A. Hill and Oxford University Press for an extract from *Advanced Stories for Reproduction*; Susan Hill and Hamish Hamilton and Penguin Books for an extract from 'The Badness Within Him' in *A Little Bit of Singing and Dancing* (1973); John Holloway and Routledge and Kegan Paul for an extract from *A London Childhood*; Laurie Lee and André Deutsch for an extract from *As I Walked Out One Midsummer Morning*; James MacGibbon, the Executor of the Estate of Stevie Smith (1957) for the poem 'Not Waving but Drowning'; Ronald Mackin and Oxford University Press for extracts from *More Varieties of Spoken English*; Jo McDonogough and Oxford University Press for an extract from *Listening to Lectures*; Colin Mortimer and Cambridge University Press for an extract from *Dramatic Monologues*; Lorine Niedecker and Fulcrum Press for a poem from *Collected Poems*; Iona and Peter Opie and Oxford University Press for the story 'The Princess and the Pea' from *Classic Fairy Tales*; Jack C. Richards and David Bycina and Oxford University Press for extracts from *Person to Person*; Saville and Holdsworth Ltd for the questionnaire on caring for and influencing people; Mary Underwood and Oxford University Press for extracts from *Have you Heard?*, *Listen to this*, and *Listeners*.

CONTENTS

FOREWORD

This series covers the four skill areas of Listening, Speaking, Reading and Writing at four levels — elementary, intermediate, upper-intermediate and advanced. Although we have decided to retain the traditional division of language use into the 'four skills', the skills are not treated in total isolation. In any given book the skill being dealt with serves as the *focus* of attention and is always interwoven with and supported by other skills. This enables teachers to concentrate on skills development without losing touch with the more complex reality of language use.

Our authors have had in common the following principles, that material should be:

- creative — both through author-creativity leading to interesting materials, and through their capacity to provoke creative responses from students;
- interesting — both for their cognitive and affective content, and for the activities required of the learners.
- fluency-focused — bringing in accuracy work only in so far as it is necessary to the completion of an activity;
- task-based — rather than engaging in closed exercise activities, to use tasks with pay-offs for the learners;
- problem-solving focused — so as to engage students in cognitive effort and thus provoke meaningful interaction;
- humanistic — in the sense that the materials speak to and interrelate with the learners as real people and engage them in interaction grounded in their own experience;
- learning-centred — by ensuring that the materials promote learning and help students to develop their own strategies for learning. This is in opposition to the view that a pre-determined content is taught and identically internalized by all students. In our materials we do not expect input to equal intake.

By ensuring continuing consultation between and among authors at different levels, and by piloting the materials, the levels have been established on a pragmatic basis. The fact that the authors, between them, share a wide and varied body of experience has made this possible without losing sight of the need to pitch materials and tasks at an attainable level while still allowing for the spice of challenge.

There are three main ways in which these materials can be used:

- as a supplement to a core course book;
- as self-learning material. Most of the books can be used on an individual basis with a minimum of teacher guidance, though the interactive element is thereby lost.
- as modular course material. A teacher might, for instance, combine intermediate *Listening* and *Speaking* books with upper-intermediate *Reading* and elementary *Writing* with a class which had a good passive knowledge of English but which needed a basic grounding in writing skills.   *(Alan Maley, Madras 1986)*

INTRODUCTION TO THE TEACHER

This book aims primarily to improve the oral fluency of the upper-intermediate learner, but attention is paid to linguistic accuracy in many of the 'Reflection' tasks. As indicated in Unit 6, fluency does not necessarily mean speaking quickly and without mistakes but keeping the attention of the listener and getting across what the speaker wants to say. Since an important part of such a skill is the meaningful use of intonation, some explicit attention is given to this in the 'Recognition' and 'Reflection' tasks.

While the focus of the book is on speaking, listening skills are obviously just as important in conversation. There has therefore been no attempt to separate listening from speaking. Some reading and writing tasks have also been included as 'pre' or 'extension' tasks. The book is particularly suitable for those students preparing for the interview in the Cambridge First Certificate Examination.

1 Classroom organization

Many of the tasks require a flexible classroom format. They assume that 'pair work' and 'group work' can be organized fairly easily. The advantages of such arrangements are that:

- they simulate the learners' experience of various types of interaction and therefore encourage the sometimes different conversational skills required for each;
- they help generate a more relaxed and co-operative classroom atmosphere;
- more students have an opportunity to speak;
- students are more likely to feel free of the pressure of being listened to by the teacher and so more ready to speak;
- students are more encouraged to take responsibility for the improvement of their performance.

In such cases, teachers are seen to be 'managers of speaking activities' rather than 'providers of instructional input'.

In classrooms where classroom furniture is fixed, many of the exercises will have to be adapted accordingly. For example, in 2.1 Task 3 the students' findings may be discussed in pairs instead of groups and in 2.3 Task 1 the talks can be given directly to the class without the preparatory group work. In some cases, teachers might be able to get some students (even pairs or groups of students) to work on some of the exercises outside the classrooom situation.

The assumption is that at this level all the work will be done in English. Students who lapse into their mother-tongue should be gently urged back into using the language they are learning.

2 Correction

If the aim of the speaking exercise is to communicate something, then correction by the teacher of grammatical error will be an unwelcome intrusion to the speaker. Teachers concerned to pay more attention to accuracy are advised either to set up a noncommunicative oral activity where the aim is for the student to display to the teacher how accurate his/her English is (e.g. using a straightforward picture story) or alternatively to note down errors for later discussion. The 'Reflection' sections encourage the students themselves to employ the latter strategy.

3 Organization

Some teachers will wish to integrate work in this book with other course work; others will use it as the sole basis for an oral fluency class. Therefore, the procedural instructions for many activities have deliberately been left unspecific to allow teachers to add, delete or alter what they wish in order to ensure the success of an activity with their particular class. Also such things as time-limits and indications as to how long an activity will last have also been omitted. These are best decided or anticipated by the teacher.

4 'Recognition'

These exercises are an essential part of this book. They direct students' attention to important conversational features in 'authentic' and 'semi-authentic' English. No attempt should be made to 'drill' these features.

The section may be organized in different ways:

- it can be completed in a single lesson or the tasks divided up over two or three lessons;
- some of it can be given as homework (tape-recorders permitting);
- the tasks which are too long or too demanding can be cut down or omitted.

As far as classroom organization is concerned:

- the teacher may have control over a single tape-recorder or the class can be divided into groups and each group given a tape-recorder;
- the work can be done in the language laboratory under the control of a teacher or on a self-access basis in a 'listening centre'.

The 'Recognition' exercises should be seen to link in with the 'Reflection' exercises. However, the latter can only be done after students have carried out a fluency activity.

5 'Reflection'

Some of these exercises simply encourage students to pay attention to what they have said and/or how they have said it. Others encourage the students to try and improve their performance.

In all cases, it is preferable if the task the 'reflection' relates to is recorded — on either audio or video tape. Discussion and analysis can then easily take place. However, during the play-back phase it is not advisable to:

- play back too long an extract;
- play it back too often (once is usually enough);
- concentrate on everything the tape has to offer.

While it is better for the *students* rather than teacher to do the analysis, teachers should be careful not to allow them to mock each other's productions or demoralize each other. This will only inhibit their performance in future!

In classes where no tape-recorder is available, teachers should encourage at least one of the students not speaking to act as an observer and take notes. Less satisfactorily, the *teacher* can take notes or the students can be asked to try and remember what was said.

Teachers are encouraged to make speaking activities both stimulating and enjoyable. Many of the exercises in this book appeal to the imagination; others are designed to provoke vigorous discussion. Obviously, anything that is likely to be either offensive or of no interest to your students should be omitted. Mostly, though, you will find that your students actively *want* to take part. Good luck!

1 Getting to know others

Task 1

Write down three personal statements about yourself. Two must be true, one false.

In groups ask each other questions quickly to determine which statements are false. You do not have to tell the truth when answering questions about the false statement. Try and catch each other out.

Task 2

Finding out

Talk to as many people in the class as possible and write down the names of at least one person who can do at least one of the following:

	Names
play the piano	
run a mile in under 5 minutes	
sew	
tell you when Shakespeare died	
speak more than two foreign languages	
swim underwater for more than 30 seconds	
explain what Quantum mechanics is	
programme a computer	
change the points in a car	

Task 3

In pairs, use as many of the following as a basis for discussion as you wish (some may not be suitable).

A Tell me about your family.
B . . . . . . Now you tell me!
A . . . .

A My birthday is . . . . . . What about you?
B . . . . . . What things do you like as presents?
A . . . .

A What do you think of school?
B . . . . . . What do *you* think of school?
A . . . . . . What are you best at?

A What do you like doing during your spare time?
B . . . . . . What about you?
A . . . .

A What sports do you like taking part in?
B . . . .
A Do you like watching sports?
B . . . .

A Tell me what ambitions you have.
B . . . . . . Now it's your turn!
A . . . .

A What things worry you in the world today?
B . . . .
A What things are you optimistic about?

Task 4

Guess the age, weight and height of three other people in your class.

Ask the person next to you whether he/she agrees with your guess.

Take it in turns to describe someone in the class. Your partner must guess who it is. Be careful not to give a name or to make the description too obvious. Include in particular age, weight and height.

2 Discovering each other's views and interests

Task 1

Tick the statements that interest you:

- Medical drugs frequently do more harm than good.
- Religion has had a greater effect on world history than politics.
- Husbands should share all domestic duties with their wives.
- The killing of seals and whales should be prohibited.
- Aid to developing countries should only be given for specific welfare and industrial projects.
- The novel is dead.
- Far from broadening the mind, travel makes people nationalistic.
- The only way the world will achieve peace is if all countries disarm unilaterally.
- Bloodsports should be made illegal.
- One day computers will rule the world.
- The United Nations serves no useful purpose.
- The family unit is the basis of society.
- Seeing a good play is far more satisfying than seeing a good film.
- All new towns should be planned as a single whole.
- Karl Marx was a great man.
- We must halt damage to the environment if we are to survive.

- Everyone should compete in at least one sport.
- Despite the changes in recent years, women are still suppressed politically and denied the best jobs.
- At school, we really only need to learn the basics of reading, writing and mathematics.
- Today's culture is pop music.
- Capitalism brings the greatest prosperity.
- When space is explored further the world will be a safer place.
- We all need to love and be loved.
- The media generally has far too much power.
- My favourite holiday is camping.
- Science offers mankind a wonderful future.
- The microchip has revolutionized the twentieth century.
- There are no such things as ghosts.
- Coal is the most valuable mineral in the twentieth century.
- Advertisers try and persuade you to buy what you don't want.
- All countries need a strong police force.
- We are all too obsessed with money.
- Most countries are very generous towards refugees.
- Beethoven is the world's greatest composer.
- Civilization is breaking up everywhere.
- I believe that visitors from outer space have landed on earth.
- Oil is a sound investment.
- We are all fascinated by stories of natural disasters.
- Parents should exert very strong discipline.
- Universities have a great responsibility.
- All waste products should be recycled if possible.

Write one word next to the statements which interest you to summarize the topic (e.g. Medical drugs frequently do more harm than good MEDICINE). Can you also think of another, less obvious, word or phrase to categorize the topic? (e.g. instead of MEDICINE you could write MISTAKEN BENEFITS).

Does the list fairly represent the topics that interest you? If not, add others. Can you put them in order of importance to you?

Task 2

In pairs, compare your lists of topics. Find out what interests your partner.

Task 3

Individually, re-read the statements on the topics that interest you and underline those you agree with. Re-write those you do not agree with so that they express your opinion.

Discuss your opinions in pairs.

Discuss your opinions with other people in the class.

3   Exploring ideas

Task 1

Look at the picture below.

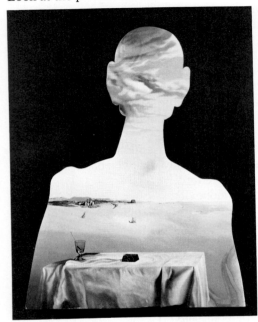

Man with head full of cloud Salvador Dali (© DACS 1986)

Listen to or read the poem as many times as you like:

Something in the water
like a flower
will devour

water
flower.

Individually write down on a piece of paper, any words, phrases or
sentences that the picture or poem suggests to you. Do not write
your name on the paper.

Task 2

With the others in your class, fold the paper up and put it in the
middle of the room. Mix up all the pieces of paper.

In groups, take as many pieces of paper as there are people in your
group and discuss the ideas on the papers. Which do you think the
comments refer to — the poem or the picture? Do you agree with
them? How do you differ? If possible, record the conversation.

Reflection

If you recorded the conversation, listen to some of it and make notes individually on the language used. Use the following headings:

Verb forms used:

Adjectives used:

In your groups, compare notes and suggest improvements where necessary.

4 Finding out about yourself

Task 1

Which of the following are true for you? If none of the answers is appropriate you may provide your own in the blank space. Compare and discuss your answers in pairs.

a How would you describe your character? Is it:

shy and reserved?
aggressive?
confident?
hesitant?
proud?
. . . .?

b What do you feel about other people? Do you:

have a lot of friends?
dislike most people?
relate better to nice people?
fall in love with aggressive people?
find most people boring?
. . . .?

c   How do you behave with other people? Do you:

    like to start conversations with strangers?
    prefer to wait until you are spoken to when you are with more
    than two people?
    dislike being touched by strangers?
    prefer to be surrounded by lots of people?
    like being on your own?
    . . . .?

d   What are your sleeping habits? Do you:

    prefer being awake to sleeping?
    sleep more than eight hours a night?
    cat-nap during the day?
    think you sleep too much?
    find it difficult to get to sleep?
    . . . .?

e   What's your sense of humour like? Do you:

    find a lot of people funny?
    laugh at jokes?
    laugh at yourself?
    find it amusing when you have an accident?
    laugh out loud when something funny happens to other people?
    . . . .?

f   Do you like talking? Do you:

    like sitting in silence with other people?
    prefer listening to people talking than talk yourself?
    talk quickly?
    like telling jokes?
    think of yourself as a chatterbox?
    . . . .?

g   What is your attitude to work? Do you:
    feel you have to keep active?
    look forward to holidays?
    find it difficult to sit still?
    hate work?
    think you are lazy?
    . . . .?

h   How much attention do you pay to your appearance? Do you:
    like buying new clothes?
    look in the mirror before you go out?
    comb your hair frequently?
    prefer wearing make-up in other people's company?
    have your hair cut at least once a month?
    . . . .?

i How practical are you? Do you:

repair things yourself when they go wrong?
feel helpless when a fuse blows?
like working with car engines?
think of yourself as a dreamer?
like making model aeroplanes?
. . . .?

j Which of the following describe you?

religious
sexy
academic
a live wire

. . . .

Task 2

Write a paragraph summarizing your partner's self-image. Show it to
him/her to see if he/she agrees. Change anything you do not agree
on.

5 Telling a story

Task 1

Look at the following pictures:

Do they remind you of a story you know?

Make notes on the story's outline. If you do not know a story, invent one.

Tell each other your stories in pairs or groups.

Task 2

Read the following story quickly:

There lived, once upon a time, a Prince, and he wished to marry a Princess, but then she must be really and truly a Princess. So he travelled over the whole world to find one; but there was always something or other to prevent his being successful. Princesses he found in plenty, but he never could make out if they were real Princesses; for sometimes one thing and sometimes another appeared to him not quite right about the ladies. So at last he returned home quite cast down; for he wanted so very much to have a real Princess for a wife.

One evening, a dreadful storm was gathering; it thundered and lightened, and the rain poured down from heavens in torrents; it was, too, as dark as pitch. Suddenly a loud knocking was heard at the town-gates; and the old King, the Prince's father, went out himself to see who was there.

It was a Princess that stood at the gate; but, Lord bless me! what a figure she was from the rain! The water ran down from her hair, and her dress was dripping wet and stuck quite close to her body. She said she was a real Princess.

'We'll soon see about that,' thought the old Queen Dowager: however, she said not a word, but went into the bed-room, took out all the bedding, and laid three small peas on the bottom of the bedstead. Then she took, first, twenty mattresses and laid them one upon the other on the three peas, and then she took twenty feather-beds more, and put these again a-top of the mattresses.

This was the bed the Princess was to sleep in.

The next morning she asked her if she had had a good night.

'Oh, no! a horrid night!' said the Princess. 'I was hardly able to close my eyes the whole night! Heaven knows what was in my bed, but there was something hard under me, and my whole body is black and blue with bruises! I can't tell you what I've suffered!'

Then they knew that the lady they had lodged was a real Princess, since she had felt the three small peas through twenty mattresses and twenty feather-beds; for it was quite impossible for any one but a true Princess to be so tender.

So the Prince married her; for he was now convinced that he had a real Princess for his wife. The three peas were deposited in the Museum, where they are still to be seen; that is to say, if they have not been lost.

Now was not that a lady of exquisite feeling?

Classic Fairy Tales Iona and Peter Opie

How does it compare with your story? Make a list of the differences in plot. Re-read the story if necessary.

Task 3

Discuss in pairs what you think the underlying meaning of the story might be?

Task 4

In pairs take it in turns to tell a traditional story from your country.

2 Monologue

1 Recognition

Task 1

Listen to the four extracts and for each one make notes in answer to the following questions:

- What can you guess about the speaker? Give reasons.
- What sort of context do you imagine the speaker is speaking in (e.g. Where is it? Who is he/she speaking to? etc.)? How do you know?
- What is the speaker talking about?
- What is the speaker's main purpose in the monologue?

Task 2

Listen again and test the statements below against each extract.

	1	2	3	4
The speaker is speaking from notes.				
The 'talk' has been organized — and possibly practised — in advance.				
The speaker speaks very logically.				
The speaker is thinking while speaking and sometimes struggles to find the right words.				
The speaker pauses because he/she is probably looking at notes.				
The style is very informal.				
The speaker is speaking very softly.				
At the beginning of each sentence the speaker's voice is at a very high pitch.				
At the end of each sentence the speaker's voice is at a very low pitch.				
The speaker uses his/her voice to get the audience's attention.				

Task 3

Discuss your findings in groups giving reasons and examples where possible. Report back to the class.

2 Persuasion

Task 1

Either
Write down three things you hate doing (e.g. swimming under-water).

In groups, exchange lists and select one item from the list you are given.

Pair up with the person who wrote it. Imagine the situation and try and persuade him/her to do the thing they hate doing. You are his/her friend.

or

Write down three objects you can never imagine yourself buying (e.g. a space suit).

In groups, exchange lists. Select one item from the list you are given.

Pair up with the person who wrote it. Imagine the situation and try to persuade him/her to buy the object they do not want. You have a large stock!

3 Giving a talk

Task 1

Select one of the following:

- one of the topics from Unit 1.2 Task 1 page 2
- the history or geography of your region/town
- your hobby (e.g. photography)
- a process you know a lot about (e.g. wine-making).

If possible, choose something the others in your class are interested in but know little about.

Prepare a 3-minute talk on your topic. Make notes and, if possible, select pictures which will illustrate your points.

If you have time, practise giving the talk by yourself and then practise giving the talk to a small group. Record each talk and discuss improvements with others in the group.

Give the talk to the class.

Task 2

In groups, discuss the subject matter of the talk. Are there any questions you want to ask the speaker? Are there opinions you disagree with?

> *Reflection*
> As a class, discuss whether the talk was formal or informal. Which formal/informal phrases did the speaker use? Did the speaker use any of the following phrases:
>
> *First of all . . .*
> *Then . . .*
> *Finally, I want to say . . .*
>
> Which features did the speaker's talk have in common with those monologues at the beginning of this unit?

4 Telling a story

Task 1

In groups, select any five objects — not people! — to be found in this picture and write them down.

Task 2

Read the problem.

An old man was looking for his lost childhood. He had wandered all over the world trying to find it but without success. One day, after what seemed like years in the desert, with the sun beating down relentlessly, he quite unexpectedly came across a huge river. On the other side he could just make out a dark forest. It seemed very mysterious and frightening to him. He could even hear noises he could not quite identify. He knew he had to cross to the other side if he was to discover the secret of his childhood. But the river was too deep and too fast flowing. He had no boat and he could not swim. Nor could he see any rocks to cling on to. How on earth did he get across?

In your groups, choose three of your five objects and explain how they might be used to tell the story of how the old man got to the other side. Use your imagination! Remember: you must choose three objects (no more, no less).

Task 3

Either
Each group mimes its solution to the class. The rest of the class should take notes and agree upon an interpretation acceptable to the miming group.

or
Each group tells its story to the class, each person in the group telling a part of it. Record it if possible. You must tell the story from the beginning. Decide in advance whether you are going to tell the story in the past, present or the future. Select your tenses carefully.

Reflection
While listening to at least one of the solutions or stories make a list under the following headings:

Verb forms used:

Nouns used:

In your groups, discuss people's lists. Correct any mistakes and suggest improvements to the way in which the story was told.

---

5   Reminiscing

Task 1

Listen to the 'old-timer' talking about his home, Honolulu, and list the changes that have taken place.

What verb forms does he use (e.g. past simple)? Compare your answers in pairs.

Task 2

Discuss the pictures below in groups. Do they stir any memories? Tell each other about the memories they prompt.

Task 3

Read the following passage. In pairs, help each other to understand as much as possible. Try to guess the meanings of unknown words in context.

Cold was an important thing in the lives of children, and adults too, in those days. I remember my surprise the first time I woke up to see the leaf patterns that the frost had made on our bedroom windows, and also the surprise of finding only a dull grey light, more like a half dark, in the veranda, because the glass roof was covered with snow. It seemed strange that snow could be so white, but make the light so grey. We used to push the snow off with a broom that we held at arm's length through the back bedroom window.

. . . . . .

When you are a child, a good deal of cold is a stimulus and an excitement: then there comes a point, either with cold and wind, or with a deep still cold, when you begin to feel afraid: you have a dim sense that experience ranges out to much greater extremes than anything you know. Once I went up alone, in the dark and the frost, on the top of a bus — most buses had open tops then. It was excitingly cold waiting for it to start; but once it was going fast, and swaying a lot as they always seemed to, the cold became sharp in quite a new way, even though I held over me the canvas cover the upstairs seats had in those days. I had to wait until the first stop before I could come down the open stairs, and I got frozen and very frightened.

. . . . . .

Although I can remember the pain of being very cold indeed, so that my ears and nose and toes and fingers used to feel a kind of cutting burning numbness, (and it hurt even more when you got warm again), I didn't want for warm clothes, and we had fires at home. Being cold in this way was simply a part of how one lived. There were long walks to do, and long waits for buses. Sometimes the buses ran very late — especially in the brown London fogs.
In the end, two or three or four might arrive together — once I even saw seven in a row — and of course the more foggy or frosty the more likely it was that this would happen. There were no bus shelters. People stamping and stomping disconsolately up and down, or hunched into their coats, were a familiar sight at bus-stops. Looking back, this seems especially so after dark: I think the evening buses were often very infrequent, and certainly they were often nearly empty when at last they did come.

A London Childhood John Holloway

Task 4

Prepare to tell your own childhood memories about one of the following subjects:

rain	bus journeys
snow	train journeys
fog	holidays
sunshine	birthdays.

Select at least three of the following words to use in your story (look up in a dictionary any words you don't understand):

horrible	thick	brother	heavy
nice	chilblains	father	dense
extreme	mother	went	pouring
handkerchief	blinding	sister	pitch
important	drenched	freezing	but
black	pleasant	friend	dazzling
filthy	like	liked	
sweat	angry	hat	
bright	slowly	gloves	

In groups tell each other your memories.

> *Reflection*
> How did you begin your reminiscence? What phrases did you use?
> e.g. *I remember once . . .*
>   *Once I was . . .*
>   *When I was . . .*
>
> What verb forms did you use (e.g. past simple, *used to, I would* + infinitive)? Was your choice similar to that of the old-timer's in Task 1?
>
> What techniques did you use to keep the group's attention (e.g. altering the volume of your voice)?
>
> What techniques did you use to signal a change in your subject (e.g. using a phrase like *Another thing I remember . . .* or starting a sentence with your voice at a much higher pitch)?
>
> If you cannot remember, ask the rest of the group.

Task 5

Write a couple of paragraphs describing at least one memory. Exchange them with someone from another group whose memory you have not heard. Read what he/she wrote and talk to that person about the memory.

1 Recognition

Task 1

Listen to the four extracts and for each one make notes in answer to the following questions:

- What information do you know or can you guess about the two speakers? Give reasons.

- What sort of context do you imagine the dialogue takes place in? How do you know?

- What is the dialogue about?

- Is it possible to say what each speaker's main purpose is in the dialogue?

Task 2

Listen again and test the statements below against each extract.

3

Talking in pairs

	1	2	3	4
The situation is formal.				
The two people know each other well.				
One person is in a position of authority over the other.				
One person is trying to convince the other of something.				
One speaker is being aggressive, the other defensive.				
The two people are talking as equals.				
At least one of the people decided in advance what he/she was going to say.				
One speaker speaks more softly than the other.				
One speaker speaks in a higher pitched voice than the other.				
Both people vary the intonation depending on what they want to say.				
One speaker interrupts the other.				
Interruptions are marked by a change in the speaker's intonation.				

Task 3

Discuss your findings in groups giving reasons and examples, where possible. Report back to the class.

2   Co-operating

Task 1

Either
In pairs, discuss who each of the following sets of biographical information might refer to:

a   Born 1893. Studied law in London. Lived in South Africa for 21 years until 1914. His commitment to Home Rule for his country frequently landed him in jail. 1946–7 his country achieved independence. Venerated as a great moral teacher and reformer. Assassinated 1948.

b   Born 1879 in Württemberg. Although Jewish sent to Catholic School. Became Swiss subject. Calculated that a clock travelling at 161,000 miles a second would be registering time at exactly twice the rate of a clock which was stationary. Died 1955 in Princeton.

c   Born 1889 in London. Joined a touring music hall act at the age of seven. Leading comedian of Fred Karno company. Made 35 films in his first year in movies. Accused by the Americans of communist leanings. Died 1977.

d   Born 1874 in Bologne. Famous discovery damaged by suspicious British customs officials. Patented 1897 in Britain. Spent the First World War in Italy. Awarded Nobel Prize in 1909. In 1929 given title of *Marchese*. All the stations of the BBC went off the air in respect when he died in 1937.

e   Born 1819. Companioned in girlhood by adults. Quickly matured. Guided by uncle: Leopold of Belgium. Married prince from Coburg 1840. Had four sons and five daughters. Popular with her subjects. Innate political flair. A lot of influence on foreign affairs. Died 1901.

Give reasons for your decisions. Tell each other more information about each person. What is your opinion of them? Compare your answers and views with other people in the class.

or
In pairs, try and match the following writers with the dates they lived. One has been done for you.

Dante	1547–1616
Goethe	1896–1940
Tolstoy	1265–1321
Virgil	1313–1375
Cervantes	1905–1980
Dickens	70–19 BC
Boccaccio	1564–1616
Shakespeare	1828–1910
Scott Fitzgerald	1749–1832
Sartre	1812–1870

Choose two or three of the writers and tell each other more information about them. What is your opinion of them?

Task 2

Write several things you know about the life of a famous person without giving the person's name. Do not worry about giving precise dates if you do not know them. However, avoid making it too easy for others to guess who it is.

Sit in groups. Exchange papers with another group.

One person in the group should read out the information on each piece of paper. Discuss each as a group and try and guess who it refers to. Add any other information you know about the person. Compare your opinions.

Join the other groups. Compare your results and discuss your opinions.

Task 3

Complete the following crossword in pairs. If possible, record part of your discussion. The clues on the next page relate (sometimes loosely!) to people's occupations.

ACROSS
1   You have to be a trained pilot to fly one.
7   These days a knife-grinder will probably find it difficult to . . . . . .
     his trade.
8   He is only a bit of an arranger.
9   What an army is supposed to do on its stomach.
12   The usherette will show you to it.
13   The astronaut landed . . . . . . the moon.
14   The so-called psychiatrist was a . . . . He wasn't even
     qualified!
15   I can't make up my mind whether to be a property developer
     . . . . . . a marketing manager.
16   He delivers the first two letters at the beginning of every week.
19   What a journalist has to get.
20   A receptionist should . . . . . . you and ask you to sit down.
21   The explorer left some of it behind at the North Pole and died in
     the snow.

DOWN
1   A musical instrument.
2   You don't expect a priest or a judge to be one.
3   A short operation.
4   Builders cover walls with it.
5   You'll have to get a mechanic to change it.
6   You're usually waited on there.
10   The beginnings of onerous work.
11   They pay particular attention to it in hospitals.
14   A barber's got to have a sharp one.
17   He'll try and cure your pet when it's unwell.
18   What you have to do to a policeman when you don't know the
     time.

Reflection
Could you describe your discussion as formal or informal?
Did one of you find more of the answers than the other?
Who did most of the talking?
Name at least one difference between you in the language you
used, e.g. perhaps one of you asked more questions.
What phrases were used to:

• make suggestions (e.g. *Why don't we* . . .?)
• express certainty (e.g. *I think* . . .)
• express disagreement.

What, if anything, did the discussion have in common with those
dialogues at the beginning of this unit?

Task 4

Individually, list the jobs you found in the crossword (in either the answers or the clues).

Put them in order to show which job you would most and least like by writing numbers 1, 2, 3, 4, etc. next to each.

In pairs, compare your lists. Give reasons for your order. Try to get your partner to change the order on his/her list.

3 Interviewing

Task 1

Discuss your present or intended career in pairs. Do you think it is involved with *caring for* people or *having influence over* them?

Task 2

Individually, circle true or false to the statements below. Now turn the page and calculate your score.

	TRUE	FALSE
I always consider other people's opinions before making decisions.	A	C
I like working with statistics.	C	A
I never hesitate to help a colleague with his/her family problems.	A	C
I frequently forget where I leave things.	B	C
I rarely succeed in persuading others when I talk to them.	C	B
Most people think I can survive being insulted.	C	A
In a new group of people I often feel anxious.	C	B
I rarely boast about my achievements.	A	C
Mundane tasks bore me.	B	C
The main aim in taking part in an activity is to win.	C	A
I am easily persuaded by the majority.	C	B
If I have a choice in the matter I do things my way first.	C	A
Success in my job is very important to me.	B	C
I like tasks which demand a lot of physical and mental energy.	B	C
I frequently ask myself how I really feel.	A	C
I make sure people that upset me know they have.	C	B

Calculate your score

Total A answers . . . . . .
Total B answers . . . . . .
Ignore all C answers.

What does it show?

A = Caring
B = Influencing

0–4 very slight interest
5–12 average interest
13+ a strong interest

If you have more A than B answers you are more interested in *caring for* people than *influencing* them. If you have more B answers you are more interested in *influencing* people.

CARING JOBS

e.g. *Medical*
doctor
dentist
psychiatrist
health visitor
radiographer

Welfare
social worker

Education
speech therapist
teacher
lecturer

INFLUENCING JOBS

e.g. *Control*
armed forces
police
prison officer
security guard

Commercial
sales representative

Managerial
marketing manager
property developer
advertising executive
market researcher

Discuss your findings in groups. Is your present/intended career the right one for you? Do you think that the statements in the questionnaire reveal your inclinations? Do you want to add statements of your own?

Task 3

In groups, devise a questionnaire to find out the careers/career intentions of another group in the class. Include both basic information questions (e.g. How many hours a day do/will you work?) and more difficult questions (e.g. Does/Will it give you job satisfaction? Does/Will it suit your character?) Start your questionnaire:

Name: . . . .

Use your questionnaire to interview someone from another group. Compare your findings in your groups. Can you select four or five things that the answers have in common?

Task 4

Either

Select one of the statements that interests you from Unit 1.2 Task 1 (p. 2). You are an expert in that topic. Sit in pairs. Tell your partner your topic.

Prepare a lot of questions which will help you find out both information about the topic from your partner as well as his/her opinion on it. Take it in turns to interview each other. Imagine you are on the radio. If possible, record the interview.

or

Select a career (not necessarily your real or intended one). Sit in groups of three. Tell each other your career. Imagine you are on the radio. Take it in turns to interview each other.

The interviewer should find out what the job is like, what characteristics and qualifications are needed, whether the interviewee thinks he/she is suitable (with reasons), etc. If possible, record the interviews.

> *Reflection*
> If you have recorded the interviews listen to some of them. If not, try and remember. Make notes under the following headings:
>
> *Intonation:*
>
>
>
> *Words the speaker could not find:*
>
>
>
> Discuss your notes and suggest ways in which the interviews could be improved.

4   Coming to an agreement

Task 1

Either
Individually make a list of at least ten factors which contribute to the successful upbringing of children, for example: a happy home life, money, a stable society.

Compare your lists in pairs and agree on one list of five factors which you consider to be the most important.

or
Which of the following contribute to the successful upbringing of children? In pairs, modify any of the statements you do not agree with so that you can both agree with them. Add any other statements you wish.

- Children should work in their school holidays and earn money.
- Parents should be strict about what time their children come home.
- Parents should not tell their children what to do after they are 16.
- Fathers should help with domestic work. It sets a good example.
- Every child needs at least one brother and one sister.
- The mother is the head of the family.
- Parents should teach boys to sew and girls to mend the car.
- The whole family (including grandparents) should live together.
- Children learn more from other children than from their parents.
- Children learn more from their parents than they do from school.
- Brothers are responsible for their sisters.

Compare your statements with another pair's. Can you agree upon a common list of statements? Remodify them if necessary.

Task 2

Listen to or read the following poem as many times as you like.

Not Waving but Drowning

Nobody heard him, the dead man,
But still he lay moaning:
I was much further out than you thought
And not waving but drowning.

Poor chap, he always loved larking
And now he's dead
It must have been too cold for him his heart gave way,
They said.

Oh, no, no, no, it was too cold always
(still the dead one lay moaning)
I was much too far out all my life
And not waving but drowning.

Stevie Smith

Look up any words you do not know in the dictionary or ask your teacher.

Help each other to understand as much of the poem as possible.

Task 3

In pairs, try and answer the following questions:

- How many 'voices' are there in the poem?
- Who do they belong to?
- Which lines are said by which 'voice'?
- What are the feelings and attitudes of each 'voice'?
- What is the contradiction in the first two lines?
- How did 'they' misunderstand the 'dead man'?

Share your ideas with other pairs.

Task 4

Either
Individually write a short poem on anything you like.

Form groups and share your poems with others in the group.

Discuss their meaning.

or
As a class, agree upon a theme for a poem.

Form groups and choose one of the following:

- individually write a poem on the theme.
  Share your poem with others in the group.
- as a group discuss what each line could be.
  Write the poem and share it with other groups.
- write a line/a stanza each and try and put them together to make a coherent whole.

4

Talking in groups

1 Recognition

Task 1

 Listen to the three extracts and for each one make notes in answer to the following questions:

- What information do you know or can you guess about the speaker? Give reasons.
- What sort of context do you imagine the exchange takes place in? How do you know? Do you know what time of day it is?
- What is the exchange about?
- Is it possible to say what each speaker's main purpose is?

Task 2

Focus on one contribution by a speaker in each extract. Say:

- who it is directed at (e.g. one of the other speakers, all of the speakers, nobody in particular)
- whether it expects a reply or is in reply to someone else.

Task 3

Find at least one example in the first two exchanges of someone interrupting somebody else. How is it done? Is there a change in the intonation? Why does nobody interrupt in the third exchange?

Task 4

Test the sentences below against each extract.

	1	2	3	4
The situation is very formal.				
The people know each other well.				
One person has more authority than the others.				
One person is directing the exchange.				
Everyone is talking as equals.				
There is no disagreement between the speakers.				
One speaker speaks more loudly than the others.				
The speakers vary their intonation according to what effect they want to have.				

Task 5

Find one example where the speaker's voice rises higher than
before. Why is this the case? Give reasons and find examples.
Discuss in groups and report back to the class.

2   Co-operating in groups

Task 1

Either
Look at the cartoons below and on the next page.

In groups help each other to understand the joke in each cartoon.

Decide what *sort* of joke it is (e.g. 'black' humour, based on
absurdity, etc.).

Discuss how international you think each joke is.

Sequence the cartoons. Which is the funniest? Which is the least
funny? You must try and agree as a group.

Compare your decision with those of the rest of the class.

"My last girlfriend could mend a puncture in half that time."

or

Read the jokes below. In groups, help each other to understand them.

- Dad, I don't want to go to Australia!
  Shut up and keep digging.
- Man: I want six slices of bacon, and make them lean.
  Butcher: Certainly, sir. Which way?
- Knock, knock.
  Who's there?
  Exam.
  Exam who?
  Eggs, ham and cheese.
- What happened to the dog who ate garlic?
  His bark became much worse than his bite.
- Waiter, is there soup on the menu?
  No, sir, I wiped it off.
- What is the French word for dentures?
  Aperitif.
- A man was at a party talking to a woman and eating salad. The man's son came up and said 'Dad, dad!' but his father said 'Don't interrupt me when I'm talking' and carried on. When the man finished he said to his son 'Now, what was it you were going to say?' and the boy said 'I was trying to tell you there was a slug on your lettuce, but it doesn't matter now, you've eaten it!'
- Life is like a shower — one wrong turn and you're in hot water.
- What's green and hairy and goes up and down?
  A gooseberry in a lift.

Can you find a joke to match the following statements?

- It is a play on words.
- The humour depends on us realizing it is an absurd situation.
- It is funny because someone is suffering.
- It is a kind of riddle.

Sequence the jokes. Which is the funniest? Which is the least funny? You must try and agree as a group.

Tell each other similar types of jokes that you know. Select the best one. Tell the other groups.

Task 2

Discuss the difference between the following:

gag	humour	play a joke (on)
practical joke	tell a joke	take a joke.

What is a 'punch line'? What happens when a joke 'falls flat'?

What makes a good verbal joke? (Can you think of an example?)

What makes a good visual joke? (Can you think of an example?)

Task 3

Try to work out the following puzzle in groups. It is not easy and you
will need to solve it logically. If possible, record your discussion.

After-dinner drink
Abigail, Bridget and Claudia often eat dinner out.

1   Each orders either coffee or tea after dinner.
2   If Abigail orders coffee, then Bridget orders the drink that Claudia
    orders.
3   If Bridget orders coffee, then Abigail orders the drink that Claudia
    does not order.
4   If Claudia orders tea, then Abigail orders the drink that Bridget
    orders.

Who always orders the same drink after dinner?

Reflection
Discuss the following questions in pairs.

- Did one person direct the discussion?
- Did one person find it easier to do the puzzle than the others?
- Was it the same person?
- Who did most of the talking?
- Name at least one difference between you in the type of
  language you used.
- Who spoke more loudly? More softly?
- How did you interrupt each other?
- What phrases were used to:
  make suggestions;
  express certainty;
  express disagreement.
- Did the discussion have any features in common with the
  exchanges at the beginning of the unit?
- Do you notice any difference between talking in pairs and
  talking in groups?

---

3   Argument

Task 1

Sit in groups. Discuss the following quotations informally for a few
minutes. Ask your teacher any words you don't know.

History is bunk.   *Henry Ford* (1863–1947)

Assassination has never changed the history of the world.
Benjamin Disraeli (1804–1881)

History is a distillation of rumour.   *Thomas Carlyle* (1795–1881)

What experience and history teach us is this — that people and governments never have learned anything from history, or acted on the principles deduced from it.   *Hegel* (1770–1831)

Poetry is something more philosophic and of graver import than history.   *Aristotle* (384–322 BC)

History is . . . little more than the register of the crimes, follies and misfortunes of mankind.   *Edward Gibbon* (1737–1794)

My argument is that war makes rattling good history; but peace a poor reading.   *Thomas Hardy* (1840–1928)

Each person selects a different quotation and makes notes which do one of the following:

- agree with it
- oppose it
- develop his/her own ideas in relation to it.

Imagine you are on radio and discussing history and its value. One person in your group should lead and direct the discussion and make his/her contributions. None of you is necessarily an expert. You have been invited as members of the public. You may take any view of history you like.

Task 2

In groups each of you select a different profession from the list below. Choose *one* only.

doctor	policeman	teacher	banker
engineer	builder	politician	scientist

Each of you has a unique skill, i.e. one that none of the others possesses.

The situation is as follows:

You are in a boat. The rest of the world has destroyed itself. You (and your male/female partners) are making for an uninhabited land to start a new civilization. The boat is slowly leaking and the only way you might survive is if two of you (and your partners) agree to go overboard to lighten the load.

In turn, present your cases to the others to say why you (and your partners) should be allowed to stay so that the new civilization can get started. If possible, record your presentations.

When everyone has spoken discuss the situation freely and try to come to some agreement as to who should go overboard.

Reflection

If you recorded the presentations, listen to some of them. If not, try and remember. Make notes under the following headings:

Words the speakers couldn't find:

Language wrongly used in context:

Discuss your notes and suggest improvements.

4   Telling a story

Task 1

Look at the sequence of pictures below.

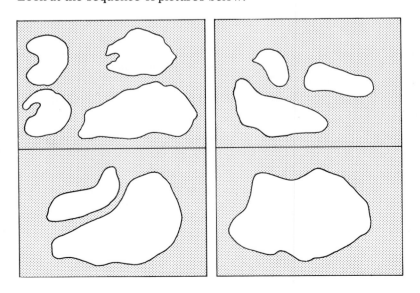

In groups, compose a ghost story using the picture sequence.

Individually, pair up with someone from another group and tell each other your stories.

Task 2

Either
Individually write up your story. Share it with your group and ask them to help improve it.

or
Write the story as a group. Discuss and suggest additions or improvements.

5

Using the voice

1 Recognition

Task 1

Listen to the story. The man is reading aloud a story which was probably written to be read silently.

Why did water come out of the barrel?

Task 2

Listen again as often as you like. On the transcript mark with a / the places where the speaker's voice pauses

e.g. some villagers/were going to celebrate/an important wine festival

It helps if you can do this on your own tape-recorder or in a language laboratory.

Some villagers were going to celebrate an important wine festival

in a few days' time, so they borrowed a huge barrel from the

nearest town, put it in the village square and determined that each

of them should empty a bottle of the best wine he had into it, so

that there should be plenty at the feast.

One of the villagers thought he would be very clever. 'If I pour a

bottle of water in, instead of wine, no one will notice it,' he said to

himself, 'because there will be so much excellent wine in the barrel

that the water will be lost in it.'

The night of the feast arrived. Everybody gathered in the village

square with their jugs and their glasses for the wine. The tap on the

barrel was opened — but what came out was pure water. Everyone

in the village had had the same idea.

Notice that each group of words carries important meaning (and therefore voice stress) usually either around a *noun* (e.g. some *villagers*) or around a *verb* (e.g. we're going to *celebrate*). In some cases it is around both (e.g. *put* it in the village *square*). Notice that when it is both a verb and a noun the stress is usually on the second of the two — in this case the noun.

Task 3

In each group, mark with a ☐ the syllable that carries the most stress, e.g.

☐

we're going to celebrate.

In some cases there may be two, e.g.

☐ ☐

some villagers.

Say why you think each stressed word is important.

Task 4

Find some groups of words where the pitch of the voice falls at the end, e.g.

some villagers

In English where the voice falls it often suggests completeness of meaning. See, for example, how many whole sentences finish with the voice falling.

Task 5

Find groups of words where the speaker's voice begins at a high pitch. There is one group where the voice begins at a much higher pitch than the others. Find it. What contrast is the speaker trying to achieve?

Compare and discuss the results of Tasks 1–5 in pairs or groups.

Task 6

In pairs, take it in turns to read sentences from the transcript trying to keep to the same pauses, the same stress, the same intonation. Comment on each other's production.

2   Coming to an agreement

Task 1

Imagine you are going to spend two weeks camping in a Scandinavian forest in July.

These are the objects you will definitely take with you:

tent
sleeping bag
clothing (except waterproofs and overcoat)
enough money for travel and basic food supplies
cooking stove

matches
plastic plates/dishes/knives/forks/spoons
a saucepan/a frying pan/cups/a kettle
toilet paper
towel

Individually, choose ten of the following items that you think you will
also need. What would be the most useful items? Think carefully
before you choose. Write out your list. Ask yourself why have you
chosen what you have chosen?

compass   books to read   a piece of string
torch   map   portable TV
sun glasses   rope   disposable bags
camera   a bottle of brandy   soap
radio   binoculars   antiseptic
sun cream   umbrella   cream
swimming costume   hot water bottle   flannel
elastoplast   overcoat   insect repellant
aspirin   pen-knife   lamp
mirror   chess set   raincoat

Task 2

In pairs, compare your lists. You must then *agree upon* one list of ten
items. In doing so, you must justify to each other why something
should be included or left out.

Move to another pair, compare and combine lists in the same way to
achieve another agreed list of ten items.

Join another group of four and combine lists. Continue to do this until
the whole class has an agreed list of ten items.

3   Describing

Task 1

Sit in pairs. Student a should look at picture **a**. Student b at picture **b**.
Individually, modify the sentences beneath each picture according to
what you can see and how you interpret the picture. Some are
obviously false.

a

Family of Saltimbanques Pablo Picasso

- There are seven people in the picture, three young boys, two old men and two baby girls.
- They are circus performers.
- They are carrying all their belongings with them.
- The girl is talking to the old man.
- The young man is sitting apart from the rest.
- Nobody is looking at anybody else; they are all looking towards something far off outside the painting.
- The woman in the foreground looks sad and lonely.
- They all look bored.
- They are very gentle people.
- The man with the cap is very thin.
- The man with his back to us is probably a clown.
- The youngest in the picture is a boy holding some flowers.
- They all seem to be going on a journey.
- The two figures closest to the viewer are seen from the back; this suggests a feeling of casualness.
- The mood of the painting is meditative and nostalgic.
- It is a very subdued picture.
- The painting is very mannered and self conscious.

b

The Arnolfini Marriage Jan Van Eyck

- It is a wedding picture.
- They are a young working-class couple.
- They are wearing their casual clothes.
- They have taken off their shoes.
- The man seems to be telling us to keep quiet.
- The scene is reflected in the mirror at the back.
- They are in the living room.
- The furnishings are very intricate and lavish.
- In the painting the room is lit by sunlight.
- The furniture is very well made.
- There is not much detail in the painting.
- It is like a photograph
- The dog is keeping away from the man.
- The man is older than the girl.
- It is beautifully painted.
- It is probably a nineteenth-century painting.

In pairs, describe your painting to each other. If possible, record part of the conversation. Compare your descriptions with another pair's and then discuss the paintings as a whole class.

Reflection

If you taped some of the discussion, listen to it. If not try to remember it.

What sort of language was used? (e.g. what tenses of verb? Were there more verbs than adjectives? What sort of adjectives were used?)

Can you find one example when a speaker starts in a much higher pitch? What is being contrasted?

Task 2

Bring in a picture of your favourite painting. In groups describe the painting to each other and help each other appreciate it.

Write a paragraph on someone else's favourite painting.

Task 3

Sit in pairs. Student a should look at figure **a** and student b at figure **b**. Follow the instructions.

Student a

Concentrate very hard on a point in the white field of intersecting lines for about thirty seconds. Then shift your attention quickly to one of the black squares. What do you see inside the black squares?

Student b

Focus hard on this negative for thirty seconds. Then quickly switch
your eyes to the blank.

Describe to each other what you can see. Try and get your partner
to see what you saw.

4   Telling a story

Task 1

Read this short-story opening:

The stooping figure of my mother, waist-deep in the grass and caught there like a piece of sheep's wool, was the last I saw of my country home as I left it to discover the world. She stood old and bent at the top of the bank, silently watching me go, one gnarled red hand raised in farewell and blessing, not questioning why I went. At the bend of the road I looked back again and saw the gold light die behind her; then I turned the corner, passed the village school, and closed that part of my life for ever.

As I Walked Out One Midsummer Morning Laurie Lee

Sit in a circle in groups of four and discuss for a couple of minutes what adventures the boy or girl might have from now on.

Task 2

Individually, take a full-sized sheet of paper and write down what you think the next line of the story could be. Do not consult.

Pass your sentence to the person on your left. Read the sentence you are given and write down the next line to that story.

Continue in the same way until you have a piece of paper with twelve sentences on it. Write an ending for the story in front of you.

Task 3

Read out the stories in your group in turn. Decide on the best. Correct the story, improve it and re-write it to make it as interesting as possible.

Rehearse the story so you can tell it without reading the paper.

Tell your story to the other groups. Tell a part of it each.

Task 4

Individually, read the following story outline:

Giovanni — journalist — landslide — Valle Ortica — late morning — no sign of anything out of ordinary — village called Goro at mid-day — square empty — landlord of hotel — 'Landslide? We don't have things like that here' — hungry but wanted to see the disaster — strange — child of twelve — 'Landslide? Of course that's higher up the valley at Sant' Elmo' — three miles — hairpin bends — valley darker and bleaker — Sant' Elmo smaller than Goro — broken down — poverty-stricken — Where was this landslide? — another boy 'Farther up. Twenty minutes away' — couldn't take car — small path — deserted — sky clouded over — 'When?' 'Three to four hundred years ago' — Giovanni furious — darker — ran back — boy in tears — stopped by old woman — 'Wait till

I call my man' — 'Come and see' — another mule-track — soon dark — peasant — small piece of land — one-third covered by crumbling earth and stones — Giovanni dumbfounded — absolutely nothing! — mistake? — mountains disappearing into darkness — back in village — well-dressed man: 'Who told you? Landslide? Rubbish!' Giovanni angry — one of the labourers: 'I'll say there's a landslide!' — 'That character has two houses for sale. Wanted to scotch stories of landslide' — Giovanni exasperated — everyone different answer — wanted big story to make his fortune — silence — church bell — Giovanni back in car — engine — lights — decided back home — nothing — smiled at absurdity — car left Sant' Elmo — steeply down the valley — not a soul — swish of gravel — headlights searched darkness — sinister crags — dead trees — engine seemed silent — initial rumblings of crash behind him — indescribable excitement — almost joy.

The Landslide Dino Buzzati

Sit in groups of four. Discuss the story for a few minutes. Discuss any unknown vocabulary.

Task 5

Divide up the story into quarters. Allocate one quarter each.

Think for a few minutes. You may make notes on your quarter but do not write out the story completely. Ask each other for ideas and clarification if necessary. You do not have to use all the words unless you want to.

Task 6

Take it in turn to tell the story, ideally without using the notes. If possible, record it. If not, make notes on each other.

Reflection
Discuss problems, errors and ways of improving the story. If possible, re-record it.

Re-tell the story — or play your recording — to at least one group and compare it with theirs.

If you can, discuss how the speakers used intonation to help them tell the story.

1 Recognition

Task 1

Listen to the man talking about fishing. This is not a written story. The speaker is probably talking from notes.

Summarize in your own words the man's view of fishing.

Task 2

Listen again as often as you like. On the transcript underline places where the speaker is obviously trying to think what to say next. They are not really pauses. How does he keep your attention?

I'm often asked why I'm so keen on fishing, and, and really I can't give a very easy answer, because why one is an angler or not is something to do with one's personality — is, it's how a person's made up. It, it's not something you learn by lifting a book and reading about it. It's something you want to do. The, there are pressures from within you, if you like, that make you do it. I think in my case it's . . . it's very closely related to the fact that I'm . . . I'm a very curious person basically; I'm always looking for em information about the universe, why things work, how things are arranged.

You know I read a splendid thing when I was quite a young angler, about fishing . . . er, er that fishing is . . . as if there were erm a . . . a . . . curtain on the surface of the water, and the angler lifts the corner and peers into this . . . rather dim and shadowy and exciting world, this mysterious world of the fish. Well I don't think it's quite a question of just lifting the corner of the curtain and looking in — that might be a biologist. I think an angler does something different. He knows what the biologist knows, of course, but he's putting his line down and putting, if you like, a . . . a line of communication down to the fish.

Task 3

On the transcript, for the final paragraph, mark with a / the places where the speaker's voice pauses. It helps if you can do this yourself from a tape-recorder or in a language laboratory.

6

Speaking fluently:1

In each group of words, mark with a ☐ the syllable that is stressed more than the other syllables. Say why you think each is stressed.

Task 4

Comment on what happens to the voice at the end of each group of words in the first sentence. Does it rise or fall?

What happens to the voice on words which are stressed (e.g. *why* things work, *how* things are arranged)? Does the voice rise or fall to make the stress?

Task 5

Does the speaker speak fluently? (i.e. not necessarily quickly or without mistakes but in such a way that he keeps your attention and you understand what he is trying to say). If so, what helps to make him fluent?

2   Reporting

Task 1

Individually, think of one thing, other than a language which you have learned in your life (e.g. to play the piano, to programme a computer).

Tick which of the following were important to you at the time. Add other statements if you wish.

How I knew what to do.

I was told.   ☐

I was shown.   ☐

I consciously watched and noticed.   ☐

I was so much in contact with it I just picked it up.   ☐

Others: . . . .

How I learned.

I tried to copy.   ☐

No-one explained or demonstrated; I just had a go;
it was trial and error.   ☐

There were clues to remind me what to do. After I knew
what to do I kept trying over and over again.   ☐

I tried systematically without help to improve my performance.   ☐

I memorized it.   ☐

I was corrected by a colleague or a teacher.   ☐

Others: . . . .

What motivated me to learn.

I *had* to learn, for a practical purpose. ☐

I wanted to show myself to be better than the others. ☐

I was encouraged to learn it. ☐

I was told to learn it. ☐

I was told to learn it or I would be punished. ☐

It was fun. ☐

I wanted to find out what it was like. ☐

I wanted to impress. ☐

I learnt it because everyone else was learning it or had learnt it ☐

It was an interesting activity in its own right. ☐

Others ....

Task 2

Sit in pairs. Interview your partner. Find out what it was he/she learnt and how it was learnt.

Report back to the class about your partner.

Task 3

List the similarities and differences between learning a language and learning something else.

Interview a different partner. Find out how he/she learnt English.

In your pairs, report your findings back to the class.

Discuss the differences between learning a language and learning something else.

3 Telling a story

Task 1

Sit in groups. Look at the picture sequence opposite.
Discuss:

- who the people are
- where they are
- what seems to be happening.

Work out a story line which explains:

- how this situation was reached
- what happens next.

Tell your story to the other groups, with each person telling part of the story.

4   Debating

Task 1

Divide into three groups at random and look at the pictures below.

Each group has a different 'motion':

Group A: Modern architecture is inhuman.
Group B: Modern architecture is exciting.
Group C: Modern architecture is sometimes good and sometimes bad. It is just a part of modern life.

Note down all possible arguments in favour of your motion. (They do not necessarily have to represent your own personal point of view.) Divide the arguments equally among the members of the group.

Task 2

Sit together as a class. One person should chair the debate.

As many from each group as possible should present their arguments.

Discuss the arguments as a whole class.

Vote on the 'motions' according to what you really believe (perhaps you have been convinced by some of the arguments) and not just because they represent your group's 'official' position.

5 Describing

Task 1

Sit in groups of three. One student should take notes about the conversation without participating in it. He/she should focus on the following questions:

- Do the speakers understand each other all the time?
- When don't they?
- Why don't they?
  Some reasons for failure might include:
- the speaker uses a word the other does not know
- the speaker's pronunciation is not clear
- the listener loses concentration
- it is not clear what the speaker is referring to.

The other two students discuss Picture A for three minutes (e.g. Who are the men? Why are they there? What are they looking at?) by making suggestions as to what is happening, fantasizing if necessary. They should then try to agree on what it portrays.

A

Task 2

All three students discuss the notes made by the note-taker.

Task 3

Change places so that there is a new note-taker.
Do the same for pictures B and C.

1 Co-operating in groups

Task 1

Look at the picture and complete the labelling.

m . . . . .

b . . . . .

s . . . . .

st . . . . .

h . . . . .

Write down as many other words as you can that relate to parts of a ship.

Task 2

In pairs, discuss what the following mean:

at the helm
crew
cargo
fo'c'sle

Compare your answers to both tasks with the whole class.

Task 3

Read the following passage and underline any words you discussed earlier.

The *Dei Gratia*, sailing from New York to Gibraltar, was fast overhauling the strange two-masted ship in front of her whose course was so unsteady she looked as if she were being crewed by drunks.

The captain of the *Dei Gratia* could see no one at the helm. He ran up a signal, but there was no answer.

As she closed in, a boat was lowered and the captain, the second mate and two men pulled toward the oddly silent ship. Then, as they rowed closer, they saw her name painted clearly across the stern — *Mary Celeste.*

The captain and the mate clambered aboard. It was 3 o'clock on the afternoon of December 5, 1872.

When they reached the deck no crew member came forward to meet them. They searched the ship from bow to stern, but the vessel was deserted.

The ship was in first-class condition. Hull, masts and sails were all sound. The cargo — barrels of alcohol — was still lashed in place in the hold. There was plenty of food and water.

In the fo'c'sle the crew's sea-chests and clothing lay dry and undisturbed. Some razors lying about were still unrusted. In the galley, pots containing the remnants of a meal hung over a dead fire.

The table in the captain's cabin had been laid for breakfast though it looked as though the meal had been abandoned half-way through. There was porridge in one of the plates, and the top of a boiled egg had been sliced off.

Everything was undamaged and in its proper place, as though the entire crew had made a sudden and collective decision to hurl themselves overboard together. Whatever had occurred could not have been very long before, because the food would have rotted and metal tarnished in the sea air.

Task 4

Write down any other words you want to know the meaning of and as many sentences as you can under the following headings:

What I know about the Mary Celeste. *What I think might have happened.*

Sit in groups and exchange what you have written. Write definitions for the unknown words on your paper and read the sentences.

Discuss what is written on your papers.

Task 5

Stay in your groups and read the next extract, underlining any words/phrases you do not understand. Help each other to understand.

The *Dei Gratia*'s captain suspected mutiny. But if there had been a mutiny how had the crew escaped? The ship's life-boat was still there.

In one cabin there was a cutlass, smeared with what seemed to be blood. They found similar stains on the starboard deck rail, near a cut that looked as though it had been made by an axe. On each side of the bows, a strip of wood 6 ft long by 1 in. wide had been recently cut from the outer planks. There was no obvious reason why this should have been done.

When he examined the ship's log, the captain of the *Dei Gratia* found that the last entry was on November 24, ten days earlier, when the *Mary Celeste* had been passing north of St. Mary's Island in the Azores — more than 400 miles west of where she was found.

If she had been abandoned soon after that entry, she must have drifted unmanned and unsteered for a week and a half. Yet this could not have been. The *Mary Celeste* was found with her sails set to catch the wind coming over her starboard quarter: in other words, she was sailing on the starboard tack. The *Dei Gratia* had been obliged to sail on the port tack.

It seems impossible that the *Mary Celeste* could have reached the spot she did with her yards and sails set to starboard. Someone must have been working her for several days at least after the final log entry. But who? Or what?

The investigation by the British Admiralty's Gibraltar office did nothing to answer the questions. The inquiry discovered that one of the barrels of alcohol had been tampered with. They found, too, that besides the chronometer, her sextant and cargo documents were missing.

They also found that ten people had sailed aboard the *Mary Celeste* — Captain Briggs, seven crewmen, and the captain's wife and young daughter. None of them was ever seen again.

Task 6

Discuss whether your ideas about what might have happened have been confirmed or disproved? Have you any other ideas?

Task 7

Read the next extract:

The explanation that seemed most reasonable at the time was the official one put out by the British and American authorities. This suggested that the crew had got at the alcohol, murdered the captain and his family, and then somehow escaped to another vessel. But the story does not really stand up. There were no visible signs of a struggle on board, and if the crew had escaped, some of them would surely have turned up later.

Dozens of theories were put forward. Had the vessel been attacked by an octopus, or some other monster which had somehow managed to extract the crew without damaging the ship itself? Or could the ship have encountered a mysterious island, newly risen from the deep? Might the crew have gone ashore, then, unable to regain their ship, drowned as the island descended once more into the Atlantic? Marginally less bizarre was the notion that every soul on board had been sucked off the decks by a whirlwind.

What do you think of the explanations? Had you already thought of similar ones?

Task 8

There was another theory put forward in 1913 about a man called Fosdyk. Does anyone in the class know the theory? Can you find out about him from an encyclopaedia? (If not, look in the Key).

2   Giving a talk

Task 1

In groups, match the stamps with the flags of the countries they come from.

Task 2

Individually choose a country from those represented that you have never visited. (If you have visited them all, choose one not represented.) Write down on a piece of paper some notes on your impressions of the country and its inhabitants (e.g. mountainous terrain, reserved character). Do not write the name of the country and do not consult anyone.

Fold up your piece of paper and exchange it with someone else in the group.

Read the piece of paper that you have been given and try to guess which country it refers to. Do the notes coincide with your impressions of that country?

As a group, discuss everyone's impressions.

Task 3

Individually, select a different country and write down what you know about it and the impressions you have of it. Find out as much as you can from other people in the class.

Give a talk to your group about the country. Tell them what interests you about it. If possible, record the talks. If not, make notes on them as they are happening.

> *Reflection*
> Focus on how the talks could be made more fluent (i.e. how the speaker could convey what he/she is trying to say without searching for words). Do not worry about mistakes or how quickly the person speaks.
>
> In groups, discuss how the speaker's fluency could be improved.

3 Telling a story

Task 1

Sit in groups of three and read the following situation:

A soldier goes off to war, leaving his fiancée behind. After five years, he returns. His fiancée has gone. She disappeared three years before and nobody knows what has happened to her. He is determined to find her.

Task 2

Make up a story based on this situation. Include in it at least three words from the following list of nouns, verbs and adjectives/adverbs.

Nouns

Verbs	*Adjectives/adverbs*
dig	ravishing
swerve	shrivelled
loathe	guiltily
flatter	courteous
concede	unconditionally

If you do not know the meanings of all these words, look them up in a dictionary or ask other people in the class.

Task 3

Agree on your story and write it out. Check with your teacher that you have used naturally any words that are new to you. Try to write as accurately as possible.

Task 4

Tell your story to the class with each person telling part of it. If possible, record the stories. If not, make notes on them.

Reflection
Try to improve each other's versions of the story.

4 Discussing issues

Task 1

In groups, select one of the following points of view for discussion.
Individually, make some notes on why you agree or disagree with the
point of view expressed and then discuss the topic as a group.

*'These days it is not enough for the woman to stay at home and the man
to go out to work. Women, too, should be able to carry on working after
they get married. Why should it be the woman who brings up the
children and carries out domestic duties?'*

*'Science gives us a better life materially. It also improves medicine and
transport. However, only art and religion can give people a sense of
fulfilment and a greater understanding of life. Science is hostile to
both.'*

*'Pop-music, commercial films and TV 'soap-opera' are either American
or American-inspired. They have so much influence they are destroying
the traditional cultures of other countries and Americanizing the whole
world. What's more, all these things are trivial. They try to exploit the
weaknesses and needs of teenagers so that their producers can make
bigger profits.'*

*'Nowadays, more people have access to good schooling. The quality of
education throughout the world is improving all the time. Teachers no
longer try to simply push facts into children unwilling to learn; they try
to develop each child's potential.'*

*'The desire for money makes the strongest of us abandon our principles.
After all, everyone can be bought for a price. Money brings powers and
it corrupts those that have it.'*

Task 2

Each group summarizes its discussions for the rest of the class. If
another group chose the same subject they should compare their
points of view.

Task 3

Each group selects a topic:

Tourism	Fashion
Racial integration	War
Unemployment	Terrorism
The role of government	Transport

As a group, prepare two diametrically opposed points of view in
relation to the topic. Write them down (maximum 50 words each) and
exchange them with those of another group.

Discuss the points of view you receive.

8

Speaking accurately

1 Recognition

Task 1

Listen to the extract. Summarize in your own words what Tim is talking about.

Task 2

Listen again. Notice that although he probably conveys what he wants to say, he does not speak in perfectly logical and grammatical sentences as he might if he were writing. This is because he is struggling to express himself spontaneously. Underline on the transcript the places where the language does not seem very well organized.

Well, I live in hope tha, that one of my ten Premium Bonds will come home. I always check the *Evening Standard* every week to make sure that, you know, wh, when I find the liver live, you know, the, the . . ., this week's winner lives in London, I'm convinced it's me, you know, [Yeah], and, erm, I think probably what we would do would . . . be to travel much more. Erm, I think we'd both continue working, but take advantage of all the spare time that we had and the fact that if you do have the money, international travel is fairly convenient, and that we could go to Africa or South East Asia for three weeks quite easily, and the only reason that prevents us from doing it now is the obvious one of cost, but more particularly if you divide the number of days you're away by the amount you're paying for, (b) it becomes quite uneconomical (Yeah, yeah) And I think obviously we'd, we'd get ourselves a higher standard of *passage de motor bike* than the one I've got at the moment, get ourselves a car, you know, and a helicopter and a few things like that, you know, the more absurd sort of things that money can buy erm, . . .

Would you stop working?

Yea . . ., no, I wouldn't. I'd go mad, I'd, I'd, it'd drive me, drive me crazy if I didn't have anything to, if I didn't have anything to annoy me, I don't know how I'd live (laughter), you know.

Task 3

Imagine you are Tim. Re-write the main points in this extract as part of a letter to a friend.

Compare your results in pairs.

Task 4

Listen to this foreign student speaking. His English is quite advanced. How organized is his speech? Is he fluent?

Note down any problems in the areas of grammar, vocabulary and pronunciation. How could what he said be improved?

Compare and discuss your findings in groups.

2   Reporting

Task 1

In groups, discuss each of the following statements. Modify them so that the whole group agrees with them:

Compare learning a first language with learning a second language.

1   Children automatically learn their first language; when you learn a second language you have to consciously learn every new word.

2   Children do not compare their first language with any other language; being able to compare languages can help an adult learn a new language.

3   Parents do not usually correct their children's language mistakes; language teachers though have to point out language mistakes.

4   Children are able to understand parents from their intonation even before they are able to understand all the words being used; students of foreign languages have to have intonation pointed out.

Task 2

A different person from each group should report back to the class on the group's view of each statement.

Task 3

Individually, tick those statements you agree with. Modify those you disagree with. If you cannot decide put a question mark.

Learning a foreign language

1   Learning English is:

- fun
- boring
- too hard for old people
- only for clever people
- easy for children
- absolutely essential in the twentieth century
- not very important.

2

English is easier for me to learn than my language is for English-speakers.

You can never really know English if you were not born in an English-speaking country.

The best way to learn English is to live in an English-speaking country.

3

- I like to learn English grammar.
- I need to translate every new word.
- I don't care if I make mistakes so long as people understand me.
- I can only learn English from my teacher.
- I like to learn about English-speaking countries as well as learning their language.
- I only want to learn to *speak* English; reading and writing are not so important.
- I like to repeat new words and phrases a lot of times until I remember them.

Compare your opinions in groups.

A different person from each group should report back to the class on the group's view of each set of statements. If possible, record the reports. If not, make notes as they are happening on how they could be improved. Focus particularly on verb tenses.

Reflection
Discuss as a class ways in which the reports could be improved, particularly in the area of verb tenses.

---

3   Giving a talk

Task 1

Form groups and look at the photographs. They were taken in
Victorian England in the late nineteenth-century.

Discuss ways in which life was different then.

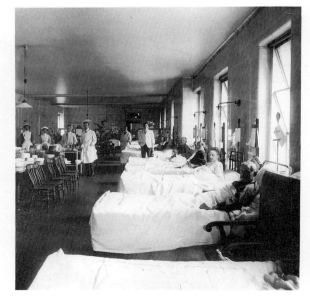

Task 2

Each group should try to select a different topic from the following:

medicine   shopping   transport   leisure   public services.

In relation to your topic, make notes on how life was different in the nineteenth century from now.

Make notes on how life generally was different in your own country in the nineteenth century. (If you come from different countries, compare and discuss your notes.)

Task 3

One member of each group should summarize the group's conclusions to the whole class in not more than three minutes.

4   Telling a story

Task 1

Read the following story opening:

The night before, he had knelt beside his bed and prayed for a storm, an urgent, hysterical prayer. But even while he prayed he had known that there could be no answer, because of the badness within him, a badness which was living and growing like a cancer. So that he was not surprised to draw back the curtains and see the pale, glittering mist of another hot day. But he was angry. He did not want the sun and the endless stillness and brightness, the hard-edged shadows and the steely gleam of the sea. They came to this place every summer, they had been here, now, since the first of August, and they had one week more left. The sun had shone from the beginning. He wondered how he would bear it.

In pairs discuss these questions:

- What time of the year is it? (Give reasons.)
- Where does the action take place?
- What time of day is it?

Make guesses as to:

- Who 'he' is.
- How old 'he' is.
- Who 'they' are.
- Why 'he' prays for a storm.

Task 2

Now read two paragraphs near the end of the story:

The fog horn sounded outside. Then, he knew that the change had come, knew that the long, hot summer was at an end, and that his childhood had ended too, that they would never come to this house again. He knew, finally, the power of the badness within him and because of that, standing close to his father's body, he wept.

They had put his father's body on the trestle, dressed in a shirt and covered with a sheet and a rug. His head was bare and lay on a cushion, and the hands, with the black hair over their backs, were folded together. Now, he was not afraid. His father's skin was oddly pale and shiny. He stared, trying to feel some sense of loss and sorrow. He had watched his father drown, though for a long time he had not believed it, the water had been so entirely calm. Later, he had heard them talking of a heart attack, and then he had understood better why this strong barrel of a man, down that day from the City, should have been so suddenly sinking, sinking.

The Badness within Him Susan Hill

In pairs discuss these questions:

- What do you now know about 'he'?
- What seems to have happened?
- How had he 'changed'?

Task 3

Make notes in pairs on a possible story line to cover the whole story.

Form groups and compare your stories. Select one and improve on it.

Take a section of the story each and practise telling it aloud. Try and get it 'word perfect'. If possible, record it. Get it as accurate as possible.

Reflection
Play the tape of your story or tell your story to the class.

As you listen to each group's story, note down mistakes and suggestions for improvement in the areas of grammar, vocabulary and pronunciation.

---

5 Reaching agreement

Task 1

Either
Individually, write down what you think the dates of the following were:

- The year of 'Revolutions' in France, Italy and Germany
- The American War of Independence
- The First World War
- The discovery of penicillin
- The French Revolution
- The death of Queen Victoria
- The conquest of Everest
- The Crimean War
- Napoleon's retreat from Moscow
- The General Strike in the UK

Sequence the list chronologically.

In pairs, compare your lists. Try to agree.

Move to another pair. Compare your lists and agree upon one.

Join another group and compare and agree on one list. Continue in this way until the whole class agrees.

or
Individually, read the following sentences. Get a rough idea what they are about:

1   I still find that people as a . . . . . . cherish the concept of their family doctor . . . . . . a friend and . . . . . ., sympathetically . . . . . in their problems . . . . . . understanding . . . . . . as 'human beings'.

2   I think it is we doctors, dazzled by the . . . . . . increase . . . . . . scientific aids to diagnosis and treatment, ... are responsible for the widespread forgetfulness of one fundamental . . . . . .: the practitioner of medicine . . . . . . ever heals anyone: the . . . . . . of healing is within the patient, the . . . . . . doctor merely . . . . . . in a natural . . . .

Summarize the main argument in two sentences. Do you agree with the views expressed?

Try to fill in the gaps. Can you say whether each missing word is a noun, verb, etc.?

In pairs, compare your sentences. Try to agree on words with which to fill the gaps.

Move to another pair and try to reach agreement with them. Combine with another group and do the same. Continue until the whole class agrees.

KEY

UNIT 3

2 Co-operating
Task 1
a Gandhi b Einstein c Chaplin d Marconi e Queen Victoria

Dante 1265–1321, Goethe 1749–1832, Tolstoy 1828–1910, Virgil 70–19 BC, Cervantes 1547–1616, Boccaccio 1313–1375, Shakespeare 1564–1616, Scott Fitzgerald 1896–1940, Sartre 1905–1980, Dickens 1812–1870

Task 3

```
H E L I C O P T E R
A . I . . P L Y . E
R . A . . A R . . S
M A R C H . S E A T
O N . . H Y . T . A
N . R O G U E . . U
I . A . I . R . O R
C . Z . E V . A . A
A . O . N E W S . N
. G R E E T . K I T
```

UNIT 4

2 Co-operating in groups
Task 3

After-dinner drink

From (1) and (2) there are six possibilities:

	Abigail orders	Bridget orders	Claudia orders
Case I	coffee	coffee	coffee
Case II	coffee	tea	tea
Case III	tea	coffee	coffee
Case IV	tea	tea	tea
Case V	tea	coffee	tea
Case VI	tea	tea	coffee

Then, from (3), Cases I and V are eliminated and, from (4), Cases II and V are eliminated. So Abigail always orders the same drink (tea) after dinner.

UNIT 7

1 Co-operating
Task 8
Fosdyk was supposed to have been a secret passenger on the ship and the only survivor. He was a friend of the captain's. He claimed that the captain had had an argument with the mate about how well a man could swim with his clothes on and went swimming round the ship. Two other men followed him. One of the swimmers gave a yell of agony. He had been attacked by sharks. Everyone crowded on a newly-built part of the deck which collapsed and they were all flung into the sea and devoured by sharks. Only Fosdyk survived.

Do you believe this story?

2 Giving a talk
Task 1
a 7 b 4 c 1 d 5 e 2 f 6 g 8 h 3

UNIT 8

5 Reaching agreement
Task 1
1848, 1775–1781, 1914–1918, 1928, 1789, 1901, 1953, 1854–56, 1812, 1926

Possible gap-fillers
1 whole as counsellor involved and them
2 amazing in who fact hardly power efficient assists process

TEXT OF THE RECORDINGS

UNIT 1

3 Exploring ideas
Something in the water
like a flower
will devour

water
flower.

Lorine Niedecker

UNIT 2

1 Recognition
Task 1

1 After the Civil War, when the Democratic and Republican parties, as we know them today, emerged, conflict was based more on the antagonism between the Democratic South and the Republican North and North East, each area vying for the attention of the mid-West and the West. Also, it was during the nineteenth century that mass political parties emerged with their appeal to a mass public via campaigns etc. The sectional nature of party support can be exaggerated, for none of the regions I have mentioned, with the exception of the South, were totally distinctive in terms of their political cultures and societies. Both parties were therefore, after the Civil War, to some extent coalitions of interests, and individual issues and personalities, and especially the personalities of presidential candidates, were certainly as important as the regional base of party support.

Listening to Lectures, Jo McDonogough
(Government Side 2 Extract C),
Oxford University Press.

2 Well, now, ladies and gentlemen, that was our last item, and all that remains for me to do is to thank our performers sincerely on behalf of us all for the pleasure they have given us this evening. And of course I must express thanks to those who've worked behind the scenes. And especially our producer. But most of all I want to say thank you to all of *you* for coming here this evening and supporting this event, especially in such weather. I think perhaps I should take this opportunity to renew my sincere apologies to those sitting in the back rows. We've made temporary repairs to the roof, but unfortunately the rain tonight was unexpectedly heavy, and we're grateful to you for your understanding and cheerful good humour. I may say that we *had* hoped that temporary repairs would suffice. But we were recently informed by our surveyor that the whole roof will have to be replaced: which is of course a severe blow when you think it's only five years since we replaced the roof of the church *itself*.

Dramatic Monologues, Colin Mortimer (No. 8)
Cambridge University Press.

3 [(...)] I am a sand modeller, a sculptor, sandsculptor, and I think I'm about the only one in the country doing work of this nature. And, erm, I started way back in about 1916, '15 or '16 I suppose, when we played on the sands, instead of having snow, which of course is practically unknown in Weymouth, we made sand-balls, made piles of sand-balls. But I found that, (you) make a ball of wet sand, take a handful of wet sand, make it into a ball, roll it into the dry sand, that draws the moisture out and leaves the ball practically like a stone. It was a common thing then for kiddies, certainly during the holidays, to pick up, erm, ha'pennies, farthings and pennies, [laughter] er, just for producing a small house, castle, fort, put soldiers on it, or even do little drawings on the, on, on a sort-of a smoothed area of sand. And, er, it amused the people walking up and down the front, and of course they dropped a few coppers. That developed, as I grew older, into larger things, er, cathedrals, churches, abbeys, and, er, and then animals — lions, groups of lions and things like that, and, er, (and) then finally a horse.

Listeners, Mary Underwood (Series B: Part 4.1),
Oxford University Press.

4 There was an Englishman, a Welshman and an Irishman and they were all due to be executed. And the firing squad brought the Englishman forward. He was standing in front of the firing squad and he shouted, 'earthquake!' and in the ensuing chaos, he managed to escape. So they brought the Welshman forward and as he was standing in front of the firing squad he shouted, 'flood!' and in the ensuing chaos he managed to escape. So then they brought the Irishman forward and as he was standing in front of the firing squad he shouted, 'fire!'.

5 Reminiscing
Task 1

This beach used to be a lot less crowded then. In those days, you could walk along here and bump into people every couple of feet. I remember, I used to sit here all alone and watch the sun go down. It was very quiet, very peaceful — no transistor radios playing rock music, no traffic noise. All you could hear were the waves coming into shore. It used to be a lot cleaner too. You didn't see any cans or bottles or junk like that — just some pieces of wood from the ocean.

The town was different too. Of course, it was a lot smaller then. There were some shops, and a few banks, and a movie theater, and that's about all. You didn't have all these fancy hotels and stores back then. And no apartment buildings, either. Most people lived in small wooden houses, painted all white and pretty.

All that changed after the war. Soldiers who were based here came back and settled down. They started to raise their families and the population grew. And then the tourists started coming — more and more every year. That's when they began to build all those hotels here — each one bigger than the next. All of them like monsters looking out to sea and waiting for the next planeload of tourists.

Of course, tourist money meant more jobs, but it also meant more roads, more cars, more pollution, *and* higher prices. Have you been to the supermarket? Have you checked out the prices? Did you know that we have the highest food prices in the U.S.? And we've also got the highest housing costs. Have you looked in the newspaper? It's unbelievable. An average person just can't buy a house here any more. You have to be a millionaire. And they call this progress. Well, you can have it. I'll take the good old days.

> *Person to Person,* Jack C. Richards and David Bycina
> (Book 1 Unit 14), Oxford University Press.

UNIT 3

1 Recognition

Task 1

1

I think it's important that we're very truthful with each other about . . . the sort of values involved, and about the priorities. I think w, we ⎰ must be care. . .

Isabel ⎱ So you have to

talk about it really?

Ray . . . must be careful to ha, yes, to be absolutely truthful about all aspects of the child, I think, and the child's upbringing.

Isabel Yes.

Ray What about the ch, what abou, what about the child's, erm, religion?

Isabel (W) That's not a problem really, though, is it?

Ray Well, isn't it? I mean, you know, ⎰ what, what . . .

Isabel ⎱ Does that, do you

worry about that?

Ray Well, I think it could be a problem, yes. I think it could be a problem once the child is born, erm, we don't follow exactly the same religion, so we will have to decide and we'll have to discuss this and . . . and, I feel that may cause a rift between us.

Isabel Do you?

Ray Well, I, I think it possibly could. What do you feel about it?

> *Have you heard?* Mary Underwood (18.3),
> Oxford University Press.

2

C.A. Good afternoon. Consumer's Association.

Susan Oh, hello. I wonder if you can help me. Er . . . I've just come back from a holiday in Greece. Umm . . . basically, I want to complain, because the whole thing was just a fiasco.

C.A. Uh, huh. Have you spoken to the tour operators themselves?

Susan Yes, I have — Xenophon Tours. I rang them this morning, and they don't want to know. I mean . . . they . . . they don't want to have any responsibility at all.

C.A. Ah, I see. Can you give me some precise details about what went wrong?

Susan Well, I mean . . . it was everything, really. I mean, the whole trip was bad. I mean, what they promised on the brochure they didn't fulfil: we didn't see Skopelos, the food was bad, the service was slow, the air-conditioning packed up . . . I mean, you know, really, it was just terrible.

C.A. Mm. Well, I suppose you therefore would have other people who could corroborate your story?

Susan Oh, yes, sure, sure. I mean, I made some quite nice friends on the boat, and I've got their names and addresses and I'm sure, you know, they would back up my story.

C.A. Mm. It sounds a rather horrible holiday!

Susan Well, I mean, no . . . I mean, Greece is great, but . . . I mean . . . the service was very bad and I think that in some way . . . umm . . . we should be compensated.

> *Quartet 1,* Françoise Grellet, Alan Maley and Wim Welsing
> (Unit 4.5), Oxford University Press.

3

David Sawer Mr Connell, I believe you're the chairman of the Noise Abatement Society. Could you tell us some of the aims of your society?

John Connell Well, our sole purpose is to eliminate all excessive and unnecessary noise from all sources.

David Sawer Mm. Is there any . . . erm . . . particular source of noise that you are . . . er . . . concerned with or that you are fighting against, for example, (I mean/ind . . .), industrial noise or traffic noise or . . .

John Connell Well, . . . er . . . there are about a hundred and one different sources of noise and we get complaints about every one of them . . . er . . . at one time or another, and we deal with about 20,000 complaints a year. Er, there are worst sources of noise, of course. I would say that the one which affects most people in most countries is traffic noise. Er . . . aircraft noise is worse in intensity but it affects only about ten per cent of the population.

> *More Varieties of Spoken English,* Ronald Mackin (Unit 8),
> Oxford University Press.

4

Policeman You say he was around average height.

Victim Yes, that's right. Around five nine, five ten.

Policeman Weight?

Victim I'm not sure. Medium, I suppose. Maybe a little on the heavy side.

Policeman Any marks on his face?
Victim No. I don't think so.
Policeman Glasses?
Victim No.
Policeman What about his hair?
Victim Black or dark brown.
Policeman Long or short? Straight? Curly?
Victim Straight, I think, and about average length.
Policeman Boy, this sure doesn't help us very much. It could be anybody. How about his clothes. What was he wearing?
Victim Well, he had a checked or a plaid shirt — you know, the kind that lumberjacks wear.
Policeman OK, now we're getting somewhere. Pants?
Victim Dark, maybe dark blue, maybe black. I'm not sure.
Policeman What kind of shoes?
Victim Boots.
Policeman Cowboy boots?
Victim No, hiking boots — brown ones.
Policeman All right, that narrows it down a little. Now I want you to look at some pictures.

> *Person to Person,* Jack C. Richards and David Bycina
> (Book 1, Unit 13), Oxford University Press.

4 Coming to an agreement

Task 2

Not Waving but Drowning
Nobody heard him, the dead man,
But still he lay moaning:
I was much further out than you thought
And not waving but drowning.

Poor chap, he always loved larking
And now he's dead
It must have been too cold for him his heart gave way,
They said.

Oh, no, no, no, it was too cold always
(still the dead one lay moaning)
I was much too far out all my life
And not waving but drowning.

> Stevie Smith

UNIT 4

1 Recognition

Task 1

1

Margaret I don't think I'm going to touch cheese or sweet or anything.
Valerie You're not?
Margaret No, I think those French beans made quite a difference. [laughter]
Valerie Just go straight on to coffee?
Manager Well, how about just . . . er, just a, a coffee, a normal coffee or would you like . . . coffee with a difference?
Valerie For example?

Margaret I'd w, a, mm, a coffee with a difference! [laughter]
Valerie Sounds lovely!
Manager Well, a coffee with a difference . . . erm . . . a . . . the well-known Gaelic coffee?
Margaret Uh-huh. That's a . . .
Manager Done with a little Irish whiskey.
Margaret And cream and [Mhm] so on, isn't it?
Manager Or something a little more exotic like a Tahitian coffee, done with rum and . . . er . . . coconut syrup?
Valerie It sounds [and cream] like a meal on its own, apart from anything else. [laughter]
Margaret No, I think I, I'm going to have a Gaelic coffee. It's ages since I had one. What about you, Valerie?
Valerie I think I'll have, I'll have some cheese, please, [Fine] and followed with a black coffee.
Margaret Just an ordinary black coffee? [Yes] Aren't you going to have something sensational?
Valerie No, I don't think so, thank you. I can still feel the Martini. It was rather good. [Mhm]
Manager We can of course, can of course, finish the whole thing off for you with Crêpes Suzettes . . . flames all over the place. [laughter] More liquor.
Valerie Oh! I wish I'd left . . .
Margaret No. I really think not. We have a lot to do this afternoon, you know, and we can't erm . . .
Valerie Yes, I'm feeling rather sleepy now.
Margaret . . . limit our capacity like that. [No] No, I think we'd better give up, you know. Erm, you've . . . seem to have, er, have looked after us very well. We've eaten very well.

> *Listen to This,* Mary Underwood (9) Oxford University Press.

2
Sarah Do you think it's a good idea for children to have television?
Lucy In moderation, I don't see why not.
Sarah ⎰ Yes, I think some people have those good
plans where
⎱ [Yes, it's]
they look through before the week starts [Yes] and they choose the programmes [Yes] ⎰ and watch nothing else.

Avril
⎱ There are some very
good programmes on for children in the mornings. [Mm] [Yes] And I think if they just watch a couple of those, then (in) say one in the e, in the afternoon, but [Yes] not sit there all day and have their meals in front of the television, I think that's very bad [and] . . .
Lucy I think it's a bad idea to say, 'You may not watch television until such and such a time, and you must switch if off at such and such a time.' On the other hand, I think just to watch it all the time [Yeah] is also a bad idea.
Mary Why? [I th...]
Lucy ⎰ Because, . . . it completely destroys
Avril ⎱ I think, no, no there are so many other things . . .
Lucy . . . all your other resources.

Avril { Yes, there are so many other things you could
      { [Doesn't]
{ be doing. And if you go and watch the television at
{ [Course it does]
ten o'clock in the morning till eight o'clock at night, that
leaves you very little time to do anything else.
Lucy   What happens the day the television breaks down?
You'd be absolutely lost. [True]

Have you Heard? Mary Underwood (17.2),
Oxford University Press.

3
A   The question of handguns always raises a lot of
discussion in this country. I'd like to get your opinions
about it. Paul, why don't we start with you? What do you
think?
B   Well, as far as I'm concerned, the law on this should
be changed. Do you know there are nearly 40,000 people
every year who are murdered with handguns? It's insane.
Guns ought to be outlawed immediately.
A   I see you have a comment on this, Jane.
C   Yes. I think people should have the right to defend
themselves. I mean, there are so many crazy people out
there. It's a very violent country, and there'd probably be
just as many murders even if we did ban handguns.
A   Roger?
D   I really can't agree with Jane. Why do people have to
defend themselves? That's what we've got the police for.
In my opinion, violence only breeds more violence. We
give people guns, and the murder rate goes up every
year.
A   Steve?
E   Well, I agree with Jane. I think people have the right
to protect themselves. If someone tries to break into your
house — and that happens all the time — you never know
what the guy plans to do once he gets inside. That's when
you need a gun.
A   Suzie, you haven't said anything yet.
F   The thing is there are something like 16,000 accidents
in homes every year involving handguns. It's not the
thieves who get killed. It's mothers, fathers, and kids.
You really should check the facts Steven. Then maybe
you'd change your mind.

Person to Person, Jack C. Richards and David Bycina
(Book 2, Unit 8), Oxford University Press.

UNIT 5

1   Recognition

Task 1
Some villagers were going to celebrate an important wine
festival in a few days' time, so they borrowed a huge
barrel from the nearest town, put it in the village square,
and determined that each of them should empty a bottle of
the best wine he had into it, so that there should be plenty
at the feast.
    One of the villagers thought he would be very clever. 'If
I pour a bottle of water in, instead of wine, no one will
notice it,' he said to himself, 'because there will be so

much excellent wine in the barrel that the water will be
lost in it.'
    The night of the feast arrived. Everybody gathered in
the village square with their jugs and their glasses for the
wine. The tap on the barrel was opened — but what came
out was pure water. Everyone in the village had had the
same idea.

Advanced Stories for Reproduction, L. A. Hill,
Oxford University Press.

UNIT 6

1   Recognition

Task 1
I'm often asked why I'm so keen on fishing, and, and really
I *can't* give a very easy answer, because why one is an
angler or not is something to do with one's personality —
it, it's how a person's made up. It, it's not something you
learn by lifting a book and reading about it. It's something
you want to do. The, there are pressures from within
you, if you like, that make you do it. I think in my case it's
. . . it's very closely related to the fact that I'm . . . I'm a
very curious person basically; I'm always looking for em
information about the universe, *why* things work, *how*
things are arranged.
    You know I read a splendid thing when I was quite a
young angler, about fishing . . . er, er that fishing is . . . as
if there were erm a . . . a . . . curtain on the surface of the
water, and the angler lifts the corner and peers
underneath into this . . . rather dim and shadowy and
exciting world, this mysterious world of the fish. Well, I
don't think it's quite a question of just lifting the corner of
the curtain and looking in — that might be a biologist. I
think an angler does something different. He *knows* what
the biologist knows, of *course*, but he's putting his line
down and putting, if you like, a . . . a line of
communication down to the fish.

More Varieties of Spoken English, Ronald Mackin (12),
Oxford University Press.

UNIT 8

1   Recognition

Task 1
Tim   Well, I live in hope tha, that one of my ten Premium
Bonds will come home. [laughter] I always check the
Evening Standard every week [laughter] to make sure
that, you know, wh, when I find the, the liver live, you
know, the, the . . . , this week's winner lives in London,
I'm convinced it's me, you know, [Yeah], and, erm, I think
probably what we would do would . . . be to travel much
more. Erm, I think we'd both continue working, but take
advantage of all the spare time that we had and the fact
that if you do have the money, international travel is fairly
convenient, and that we could go to Africa or South East
Asia for three weeks quite easily, and the only reason that
prevents us from doing it now is the obvious one of cost

but more particularly if you divide the number of days you're away by the amount you're paying for, it becomes quite uneconomical. [Yeah, yeah] And I think obviously we'd, we'd get ourselves a higher standard of *passage de motor-bike* than the one I've got at the moment [laughter], get ourselves a car, you know, and a helicopter and a few things like that, you know, the more sort of absurd things that money can buy, erm, . . .

Beryl Would you stop working?

Tim Yea . . . , no, I wouldn't. I'd go mad, I'd, I'd, it'd drive me, drive me crazy if I didn't have anything to, if I didn't have anything to annoy me, I don't know how I'd live [laughter], you know.

Have you Heard? Mary Underwood (19.3), Oxford University Press.

Task 4

Interviewer Um, Peter, where do you come from?

Peter I come from Zurich, the German, from the German-speaking part of Switzerland.

Interviewer And could you tell me a little about your background. Er have you finished school now?

Peter Yea, before I came here I have just finished high school and, er you mean, I shall tell you something about my family?

Interviewer Well, yes . . . erm well, no . . . I was thinking about . . . Did you learn English at school?

Peter Yea, I had er only a facultative course of English because I er learnt er the classics, Latin and Ancient Greek, and so I thought this is the right moment to come to England to learn . . . English.

Interviewer Yes, and, when you say er you only did a little English at school, how many years did you do?

Peter Oh, it was only for two years and not very regular. . .ly.

Interviewer Right. And how often a week?

Peter It was er one hour, one lesson a week mm but, er as I said before, it was, it was nothing special.

Interviewer Not a lot.

Peter I didn't, I didn't learn very much.

Interviewer Yes. So you decided to come to England?

Peter Uhmm.

Interviewer And is this the first time you've been?

Peter No, I've been to England er one year ago but only in London and, er of course, this is something completely different—to stay in er England for eleven weeks as I do.

Interviewer So this is your first, um, the first time you've actually been studying in England?

Peter Yea.

Interviewer And um have you been doing all your classes in English?

Peter Um.

Interviewer Or have you been doing . . . You've been at a language school?

Peter Yea.

Interviewer And so all your studies have been in learning English?

Peter Yea, just . . . I was concentrating on learning English.

Interviewer And have you enjoyed it?

Peter Yea, I have, I have to say this, yea, really, I enjoyed it, and er I, it was my target to learn English so that I can go to a cinema and understand what's going on, and er to watch TV and to understand what they are speaking about, and er also I can read now a book without too many difficulties.

Interviewer So in fact you've reached your, the target you set yourself?

Peter My first target, yea.

Interviewer Um, what would you say that you're good at doing in English?

Peter Pardon?

Interviewer What would you say you're good at doing in English?

Peter Um.

Interviewer Reading or speaking?

Peter I think during this eleven weeks I stayed here, I've stayed here er I improved very much my er written er English and er reading comprehension so, as I said before, um, I can read a book or so without too many difficulties. Er the thing about my, the speaking, the spoken language is that, er um, I, you need a certain time to adapt er the words you wrote you read to, to use them in your spoken language. Of course, it's er that takes a certain time and er so its goes slowlier. [Yes, yes.] more slowly.

Interviewer Do you actually think you make a lot of mistakes when you speak? I'm not saying you do, but do you think you do?

Peter Yes, sometimes er I realize after, er I don't know, after a part of a second that it was wrong what I said or I realize it a little bit later if er my counterpart is answering the question and er of course I am doing mistakes without knowing about because I'm still thinking in German [Hmm mm] and er so I think this, um, con. . . this construction has to be right or . . . is er I think in this German way and translate it, and anyway it's impossible for me to realize it, er that it's wrong.

Interviewer Erm do you like people correcting you or does it irritate you or put you off?

Peter I think, er, of there are different em conversations sometimes. If you speak with another language student about er we are something which is very important for you and er you speak about er your plans or your girlfriend I, I don't . . . then er it would be silly to er correct each other, but er if you are speaking about the politics or so or what's going on in economics, then er of course er I, I don't mind if someone is correcting me. I think it's good. Yeah.

Interviewer And one final question. Now you're going back home, how are you going to keep your English up?

Peter Er, I'm sure I'll read a lot in English. I've bought a lot of books and I so I have er some stuff to . . . I don't know, perhaps, um, I have also the possibility to watch TV with the Sky Channel or so. Until now we have no TV at home but er perhaps in next year or so we'll buy one.

Interviewer Thank you very much. Good luck.

Peter Thank you.